It's a Party!

THE NIGHT SHALL BE FILLED WITH
MUSIC & THE CARES THAT INFEST
THE DAY SHALL FOLD THEIR TENTS
LIKE THE ARABS & STEAL
AS SILENTLY AWAY.
—HENRY WADSWORTH
LONGFELLOW

SUSAN BRANCH

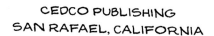

CEDCO PUBLISHING
SAN RAFAEL, CALIFORNIA

CONTENTS

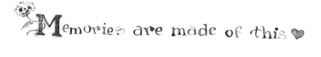

Memories are made of this ♥

A party is truly a gift from you to your friends — it's a chance to show them you love them — en masse! Life can always use a little spicing up, so give a party! Appeal to the senses — just name them off to yourself & see if you have provided for each: does it LOOK good? (fresh flowers, soft lighting, lots of candles, festive decorations); does it SOUND good? (crackling fire, ticking clocks, wonderful music); will it TASTE good? (plan the food: have crunchy & smooth, sweet & tart — make it colorful); does it FEEL good? (turn the heat a little lower than usual, give lots of hugs ♥); does it SMELL good?

4

…ERFUL ✦ PARTY ✦

(things cooking, perfume & flowers, a gardenia 🌸 pinned to your shoulder); & then the MAGICAL 6th sense — IMAGINATION: maybe some games, a violinist or piano player, 🥂 ribbons tied to the wine glasses, 🎀 luminarias or a lit pumpkin cut all 🎃 over with stars on the front porch for welcome.

There are a million good reasons to have a party — you can have a theme; it can be a big blow-out New Year's party, a cozy football & song party, a lunch, brunch, dinner, or tea — keep a camera nearby &

HAVE A WONDERFUL TIME !

THEY ARE NOT LONG, THE DAYS OF WINE & ROSES. *Ernest Dowson*

Life is a cabaret old chum, Come to the cabaret...

A little nonsense now & then
is relished by the wisest men.
and women ♥

PARISIAN TAXI

1 PART STOLI VANILLA VODKA
1 PART TIA MARIA
2 PARTS STRONG COFFEE OR
ESPRESSO, DECAF OR NOT

CHILL ALL INGRED. SHAKE WITH ICE &
STRAIN INTO GLASS RIMMED W/ SUGAR
OR CINNAMON·SUGAR. (RIM GLASS W/ VODKA
& DIP INTO SAUCER FILLED W/ SUGAR.) ♥

WATCH
OUT
FOR HIT AND RUN!

Kahlúa Shake

2 10 oz. servings

Frothy & fun. ♥
Perfect after summer
sports. ♥

2 oz. Kahlúa
2 oz. vodka
1 c. milk

3 scoops vanilla
ice cream
crushed ice
large straws

TOP WITH A CHERRY

Put Kahlúa, vodka, milk & ice cream into blender. Blend on high speed for about 35 seconds. Fill 10 oz. glasses half way with crushed ice; pour in Kahlúa mixture; stir well.

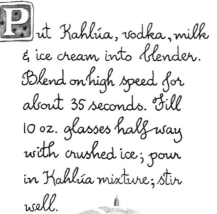

Add straws & serve. ♥

COSMOPOLITAN

1 PART VODKA
1/2 PART TRIPLE SEC
1/4 PART ROSE'S LIME JUICE
2 PARTS CRANBERRY JUICE

SHAKE WITH ICE & STRAIN INTO
A MARTINI GLASS. GARNISH WITH
A THIN SLICE OF LIME.

PAINT THE TOWN A
HOT, BABY-GIRL,
BUBBLE-GUM
Pink

ICED VODKA WITH

This is so beautiful at a party & it only gets prettier as the ice melts and the rose petals begin to stick through. ♥

1 bottle good Russian vodka
1 clean, empty, narrow bottle with a long neck, and a top
1 clean, empty, ½ gallon milk carton, with the top cut off, or just opened up
6~8 sweetheart roses
extra greenery, like box or rosemary, if you like

SWEETHEART ROSES

Funnel the vodka into the bottle, cork it, and set the bottle into milk carton. Fill to neck with water & surround with roses & greenery — arranging as best you can, unfolding leaves; everything totally under water. Freeze it (vodka doesn't freeze). When it's time to serve, peel off milk carton, & set into rimmed bowl with more greenery.

Gorgeous, eh? ♥

15

PLAY

AND HAVE FUN

At the end of the day, pour yourself something cold & frosty, head for the porch, put your feet up & smell the roses. What's it all for if we don't take time to kick back & enjoy the fruits of our labors? ♥

COME AND PLAY. WE'LL BE

C E L E B R A T E

SPONTANEITY IS A WONDERFUL THING, SO IT'S ALWAYS GOOD TO PLAN FOR IT! YOU PUT YOUR DENTIST APPTS. ON THE CALENDAR ~ HOW 'BOUT FUN? 💙

FRIENDS FOR-EVER-MORE.

JELL-O SHOOTERS

P ass a plateful to partygoers;
they almost feel like sin, but it's
only Jell-O made dangerous!

1 6 oz. pkg. Jell-O (red or blue)
1 pkg. Knox gelatine (2 tsp.)
1 1/3 c. vodka or rum
2/3 c. cold water

Add 2 c. boiling water to Jell-O &
gelatine ~ stir 2 min. Stir in vodka & cold
water; pour into 9" x 9" pan. Chill until set.
Cut into squares. (Shoot in moderation.)

Skip & Go Naked

Fill a blender half way with ice.
Add 2/3 C. cold beer, 2/3 C. frozen
pink lemonade concentrate, 1/4 C. vodka.
Blend well, serve. ♥ Makes 2 big drinks.

THE MOON ♪
BELONGS TO
EVERYONE— ♫
THE
BEST THINGS IN
LIFE ARE FREE

HULA GIRL

THIS HAS MANY REDEEMING
QUALITIES: A BANANA FOR
INSTANCE, & JUICE!
MAKES 1 BLENDER-FULL

3/4 C. RUM
1/2 C. MANGO JUICE
1/2 C. PINEAPPLE JUICE
2 TB. GRAND MARNIER
1 WHOLE RIPE BANANA
FRESH LIME
NUTMEG

PUT 1ST 5 INGRED.
IN BLENDER, FILL
W/ICE; BLEND
WELL. POUR INTO
GLASS W/ A SQUEEZE
OF LIME & A SPRINKLE
OF NUTMEG. PREPARE
GLASSES: RUB RIM
W/LIME JUICE & DIP INTO COLORED
SUGAR. SERVE W/ A PARASOL. ♥

21

A toast to us my
good fat friends,
To bless the
things we eat;
For it has
been full many
a year, Since
We have seen
our feet: Yet
who would lose

a precious pound,
By trading
sweets for sours?
It takes a mighty
girth indeed,
To hold such
hearts as ours!

 Wallace Irwin

I'LL DRINK TO THAT

CHOCOLATE
MINT COFFEE

♥ ♥ ♥

The perfect way to end an evening. ♥
Serves 4

½ c. whipping cream
2 Tbsp. powdered sugar
1 tsp. vanilla
1 oz. German sweet chocolate—grated
2 c. strong hot coffee
8 Tbsp. peppermint schnapps
chocolate curls

Beat cream with sugar & vanilla until soft peaks form. Fold in grated chocolate. Pour hot coffee evenly into 4 mugs & add 2 Tbsp. schnapps to each. Spoon on whipped cream.

Garnish with chocolate curls & serve immediately. ♥

Only Irish coffee provides in a single glass all four essential food groups: alcohol, caffeine, sugar & fat.

♥ Alex Levine

SWEET LORETTA
Mudslide

1 PART ABSOLUT VODKA
1 PART KAHLUA
1 PART BAILEY'S IRISH CREAM
(1 PART KISS YOUR HINEY GOOD-BYE)
1 SCOOP VANILLA ICE CREAM

PUT EVERYTHING INTO A BLENDER W/LOTS OF ICE. POUR INTO A GLASS RIMMED IN CINNAMON-SUGAR. (RUN WET (KAHLUA) FINGER AROUND RIM OF GLASS & DIP IT IN CINNAMON-SUGAR.)

I'M AS PURE
AS THE
DRIVEN
SLUSH.

Tallulah
Bankhead

PEACH CREAM

Tastes like a Creamsicle. ♥

1 oz. peach schnapps
1 oz. fresh orange juice
2 oz. vanilla ice cream
½ c. crushed ice

For each drink, put all of the above in a blender & blend 30 seconds. Serve. ♥

AN APPLE IS AN EXCELLENT THING—
UNTIL YOU HAVE TRIED A PEACH. ♥ GEO. DU MAURIER

GOD RESPECTS ME WHEN I WORK, BUT HE LOVES ME WHEN I SING. ♥ RABINDRANATH TAGORE

On with the dance!
Let joy be unconfined.
💜 Lord Byron

CHAMPAGNE COCKTAILS

These are absolutely yummy ~
Contrary to one's first reaction, there
is little chance of becoming addicted
because the aftereffects can be
totally devastating.
But oh, what
a
night!

Chilled champagne glasses
Good-quality champagne
Sugar cubes
Angostura bitters

Soak the sugar cubes in the bitters.
Drop one cube in each chilled
champagne glass and fill with
champagne. Serve.

31

A TOAST TO YOU...

May you live to be a hundred years,

WITH ONE EXTRA YEAR TO REPENT.

♥ Old Irish Toast